CHI

ENERGY

Activation, Cultivation and Flow

(Clear's Tai Chi Book I)

by Richard E. Clear Jr.

CHI ENERGY
ACTIVATION, CULTIVATION AND FLOW

Copyright © 2005 Richard E. Clear Jr.

For information contact,

Clear's Silat Street Kung Fu
113 E. Broadway Ave
Maryville, TN 37804

Phone
(865) 379-9997

Websites

www.clearstaichi.com

www.clearsilat.com

Dedication

This book is dedicated to
my wife Muriel and my son Chase
because they have taught me
so much
about unconditional love, willpower and
making life fun
but most of all about love.

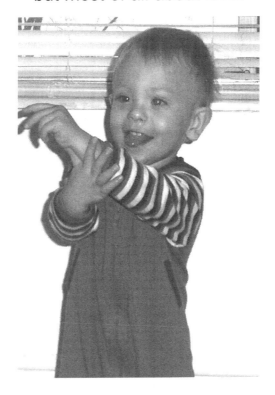

❧ I Corinthians 13 ❧

WARNING!

This is an instructional book on Chi Kung energy and related practices and as such is intended to be an aid to properly supervised instruction. Improper or incorrect practice of Chi Kung can cause physical, mental and/or spiritual damage. We recommend that these arts be learned and practiced only under the guidance of a certified instructor.

The author and publisher of this material are not responsible in any manner whatsoever for any injury which may occur through reading or following the instructions in this book. It is essential that before following any of these activities, physically or otherwise herein described, the reader should consult his or her physician.

Table of Contents

INTRODUCTION

In this book I am explaining some real first level advanced practices regarding Chi/Qi/Ki Energy activation, cultivation and flow that will allow the average person to experience Chi for themselves. I am also putting forth a basic definition of the word Chi and some related Chi terms. It is my hope that you will benefit from this information and seek a deeper understanding and practice of Chi Energy for the many benefits that it can provide to you and to others.

THE CHI DEBATE

In the West many debates have surrounded the idea of Chi and if Chi really exists. Chi is a Chinese word that when simply translated into English means Energy and or Life-Force. The debate(s) typically starts around the so called manipulation of the chi life force energy. Often, these skills are seen demonstrated by advanced masters during cultural events, festivals or demonstrations etc. Unfortunately, to the average person these skills then appear to be similar to a circus sideshow or magic tricks where trickery or illusion and sleight of hand are involved. Also, many of the techniques of Chi

2

Energy activation and cultivation have been kept secret so little explanation for the seemingly impossible feats of skill are offered and this adds to the idea that some kind of illusion is behind the skills being presented and/or demonstrated. Much of the secrecy is due to specific groups (religious or trade guilds) or families having a history and tradition of skills and practice that is supposed to be kept within the group or family and not revealed to outsiders. This is a part of the heritage and cultural phenomenon of the Chinese people and only in very recent years have these practices begun to come into the modern world of scientific exploration, methodology and measurement. Most modern Masters of the arts agree that all chi phenomena can be explained and fits well within the realm of modern physics. So, after many years of study and teaching it is my personal feeling that really it is the idea of mind over matter that is at the heart of the debate.

There are other factors that compound the problem of understanding the reality of Chi activation, cultivation and flow. The first problem to be addressed is a language barrier. There are words that describe specific aspects of Chi and Chi Kung (Energy Work) practice for which there is simply no direct translation into English and often Chinese teachers of Chi Kung aren't proficiently fluent in English like a native speaker so although they may know some English there is still a communication barrier. Another issue to be addressed is that some of the historical background on many of the practices are based on specific exercises and postures that were created to facilitate specific energetic processes and little explanation other than to just do the exercises is commonly taught to beginners.

High level Chi Kung skills like so many other advanced practices can require years of dedication and practice to develop and many potential students of Chi Kung start because they see a demonstration or hear about a high level skill and desire to learn it. Unfortunately, many Chi Kung teachers feel that the beginner must earn the right to learn the real material and see little reason to give any incentive to the beginner. So, often training begins with a simple practice that does not contain any real immediate Chi activation so when the first practice is to stand in one place and breathe every day for several months or longer or practice the 8 postures without any incentive many *would be* Chi Kung Masters simply quit due to not understanding or not having enough patience for the traditional process. As a result there are few truly skilled Westerners in this art form. We feel it is time for this situation to change.

We are pleased to offer a text for Westerners to get a real glimpse and basic understanding into the practices of Chi activation, cultivation and flow that will give the practitioner enough knowledge and incentive to advance their studies in this fascinating discipline. We offer various programs and workshops in Chi Energy training from beginner to advanced and much of what is in this text is at the beginning of many of our programs. The information in this book applied to Tai Chi, martial arts or energetic arts of any kind will greatly aid and benefit those practices. We hope you enjoy this book and that it begins or adds to your journey in the Mind Body and Spirit Healing Arts.

REQUIREMENTS FOR SUCCESS

The number one ingredient for success is desire. An equally important ingredient for success is commitment and perseverance. Belief is a helping factor but not a requirement for this system of Chi Kung.

It is commonly thought that belief is a requirement for success and I intentionally have sought out and practice methods that work even if belief is not present. If a delusional person believes that they can jump off the top of a 50 story building and land on concrete without getting hurt and then they jump then the most likely result is that they will end up dead and their body will be a mess on the street below. If the average somewhat inactive person does not regularly walk and do push-ups and then starts walking and doing sets of push-ups every day, in moderation, then typically they will have a positive benefit over time even if they start out believing that the walking and push-ups will not have an affect. In both of these situations belief may help in the situation but it is not required for an affect to occur.

The main thing to believe when learning Chi Kung is that many things are possible and that opens up the door to focus on how to achieve the result. People can fly! Does this statement seem outrageous? At one time this was thought to be impossible. Now it is hard to go anywhere and not see an airplane in the sky. However, before the first balloon and airplane flight people who were completely closed off from the possibility that people could fly would not even consider how the feat could be accomplished let alone ever try to make it happen. If you really don't believe a thing is possible then you will almost certainly fail at it no matter how hard you try because you are fighting against your own mindset and beliefs.

There are many examples in our society of people doing seemingly impossible feats. While some feats are tricks or illusions there are many that are simply a matter of a person applying a great amount of willpower and dedication to achieve the desired goal. This is true with anything from figuring out a way to fly to the first time a human being was documented achieving the ability to run a mile in less than 4 minutes. Everyone thought this was impossible until it was done by Roger Bannister in 1954. Once this feat was accomplished many others also ran a less than 4 minute mile. For most of the people who accomplished the feat it took real belief in the possibility first. Belief was not as difficult once someone else had done it. However, each person must still overcome their personal obstacles to accomplish such a feat. There are also examples of ordinary non-trained people doing what seems to be the impossible in a moment of crisis, such as lifting a car off of a loved one who is trapped underneath.

Last but not least critical thinking is always recommended. Do not just blindly believe anything and everything that comes your way. Be willing to try new things but scrutinize, analyze, critique and consider the possibilities and causes of what you do, feel and experience. This will help you to achieve real success and take your personal abilities to higher and higher levels.

TRADITIONAL CHINESE MEDICINE

TCM

In Chinese medicine there are at least five different primary methods of healing and there are numerous other lesser known methods of healing. The main five methods of healing are acupuncture, herbology, Chi Kung, bone setting and tuina massage. Each of these methods has many subcategories, methods and different schools of thought.

YIN & YANG
BALANCE = UNITY OF POLAR OPPOSITES

TCM utilizes Chi and Yin and Yang theory. The basic idea as applied to Chinese Medicine is that balance is the proper state of health. Yin and Yang are polar opposites that are partly defined by each other such as big and small, fast and slow, hot and cold, action and stillness, light and dark, up and down, wet and dry etc.. If there is imbalance in the body, mind or spirit such as to much heat or to much cold then it is unhealthy and sickness will result. The goal of healing with TCM and healing Chi Kung is to restore, regulate and maintain Chi balance to the mind, body and spirit.

Yin and Yang theory is one of the least understood aspects of TCM by most Westerners because it is variable and not fixed. For example: Earth is Yang and Water is Yin. However, either can be yang/hot or yin/cold. Compared to hot water steam is Yin or light even though it is in a hotter (more yang) temperature state than the liquid hot water. Ice is more yang than cold water because it is harder than liquid water even though by virtue of the temperature it is in a colder (more yin) state. Fifty degree air temperature is yin compared to 100 degrees but is yang compared to 10 degrees.

ACUPUNCTURE MERIDIANS AND POINTS

The largest and most common school of thought in TCM (Traditional Chinese Medicine) utilizes *meridian* and pressure point theory. Meridians are invisible pathways in the body much like the nervous system that carries electrical pulses and stimuli except the meridians are thought to be channels or pathways that Chi energy flows through. Where the meridian lines can easily be accessed from the body surface is where most of the pressure points are located. Quite often pressure points are located in the same vicinity of the body where a blood artery or large vein and large nerves or nerve bundles are near the surface of the body.

If you look closely at most acupuncture charts you will usually see the meridian lines on the chart and the pressure points are on the lines.

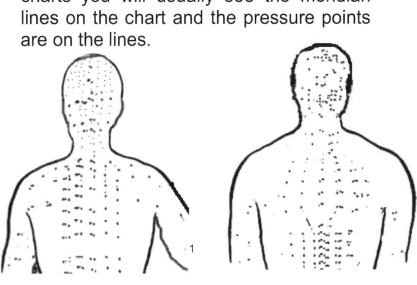

Most acupuncturists will first talk with the client/patient and have the patient fill out a questionnaire in much the same manner as a regular Western medical office. Then, the acupuncturist will do at least one version of Traditional Chinese Medicine diagnosis. There are many different diagnosis methods including but not limited to looking at the tongue or eyes or end of finger tips but the most common traditional method is Pulse diagnosis. Advanced masters can diagnose by sight.

To perform pulse diagnosis the acupuncturist will place their fingers on the palm side of the wrist and feel the energy flow through the soft tissue of the wrist. The sensations being felt for are a fast, slow, extra strong or extra weak pulse in one or the other of the meridians. Also, the practitioner is feeling for heat/dryness or wetness and/or any sensation that distinguishes one meridian from the others. Any difference in sensation indicates an imbalance in one or more meridians which in turn reflect physical problems or maladies. The idea in acupuncture is that by adjusting the meridians the physical state should also improve. A very sensitive touch is required to diagnose this way but it is simply a matter of practice to learn it.

Once the diagnosis has been made then the acupuncturist will consider the treatment options and insert the needles into the correction points. Then, the TCM physician uses sensitive touch once again to turn and adjust the needles so that they are influencing the flow of Chi through the meridians and hence adjusting the Chi flow through the entire body. Multiple follow-up treatments may be required to get the body to go back into balance and to fully accept the chi flow adjustment.

Historically, in China once the needles have been inserted into the patient then the TCM practitioner will influence the chi flow by using their hands and fingers to direct chi through the needles without touching the needles or the patient. This method is rarely practiced today as most practitioners do not have the knowledge or skill required to properly do it. Also, the Chi flow can be directed without needles. Using energy to direct the flow of Chi is taught in our more advanced programs.

DEFINING CHI

CHI = ENERGY

Simply translated and defined Chi means energy. **Merriam-Webster dictionary online defines energy as usable power (as heat or electricity);** *also*: **the resources for producing such power.** The energy that Chi refers to can be explained in many ways including but not limited to electricity, magnetism, gravity, sunlight, atomic particles such as oxygen and hydrogen, the nutrients and biological energy of food, genetic materials and information received from our parents and even the energy of thought, belief and prayer. The specific energy Chi refers to is Life-Force, vital force, intrinsic energy, spirit and breath. This life force is a combination of *pre-birth Chi* which includes the genetic material received from your parents and *post-birth Chi* or energy gained after you are born which includes the food you eat and the energy you gain through sleep and deep breathing exercises etc.

CHI = LIFE FORCE

One of the more common problems with discussing the word Chi is separating the term from its application. Many skeptics argue that Chi does not exist. However, they tend to agree that energy does exist and that our body is made up of tiny particles that are energy in some form. The skepticism or disbelief that exists is regarding the fantastic and superhuman feats that get demonstrated regarding the use or directing of Chi by an individual. This includes such things as breaking hard materials such as boards and bricks, taking massive hits to the body without injury, diagnosing and healing others with bio-energy with or without physical contact, moving people with energy without physically touching them and other feats that are typically more associated with psychic ability. In the following text will be simple but powerful exercises designed to help the average person Activate and feel their own Chi flow. These same exercises will also allow the practitioner to cultivate the Chi energy or Life Force. Life Force in the West is commonly thought of as spirit and interestingly the physics law/idea that energy does not die but changes form is a shared concept between the East and the West. Both cultures believe that when a person physically dies the Chi – Life Force – Spirit leaves the body.

CHI = SPIRIT

At this point in the reading you may be wondering what is Chi specifically. Again the simple translation is Energy with all of the possible connotations of that word. Multiple books could be and have been written on any one aspect of energy. Many books have been written on just electricity and magnetism. Many books and articles have been written on gravity and effects of gravity. Electricity, magnetism and gravity are only three types of energy out of the many different types of energy that exist. So, what is of interest here is how the science and art of the Chinese concept of bio-electro-magnetic mind and spirit energy can be studied, developed and applied.

CHI KUNG = ENERGY WORK

Chi translates as Energy. Kung translates as Work. Kung Fu translates as Work Skill or Great Skill attained through hard work. There are different types of Chi Kung. There are farmer's exercises which are mostly just to keep the body strong. There is Chi Kung for health to keep the body young and healthy. There is also Chi Kung for mind development and Chi Kung for self defense/fighting.

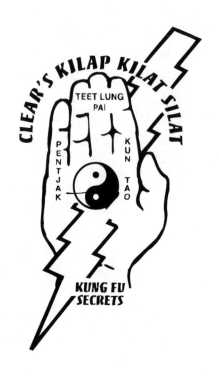

CLEAR'S KILAP KILAT SILAT

TEET LUNG PAI

PENTJAK

KUN TAO

KUNG FU SECRETS

MIND INTENT & ENERGY EXPRESSION

THE MIND DETERMINES ENERGY EXPRESSION

The mind determines energy expression. The physical expression of Chi energy is referred to as Jing. This can occur by conscious direction or automatically without consciously directed thought because the state of the mind still causes the jing response. For example, when someone becomes angry or fearful they may experience tension and changes in blood pressure and blood flow as well as adrenaline release all of which are going to affect the way the person is experiencing and expressing energy. The physiological response may have already started before the conscious mind realizes what is happening. One of the goals of high level practice is to become much more aware of the conscious and unconscious mind and mental state and to direct Jing in a highly refined way as wanted and needed.

Emotional Mind Intent is called Shen. To consciously direct energy Mind Intent is needed to make the decision to determine the form and direction that an individual's energy will take. Sometimes this will involve a constant mental effort but often once a decision is made (consciously or unconsciously) the energy will tend to follow the direction as long as the energy is available and there is no conflicting tension, information or direction.

Yɪ = Intellectual Mind Intent

There are several different kinds of Mind Intent. The primary type of mind intent we are utilizing in Tai Chi and in the Chi Kung exercises presented in this book is Yi or I (pronounced ee). Yi translates as Intellectual Mind Intent. In most Yi exercises the mind, body and spirit are calmed and through proper relaxed mental focus or/and specific physical alignment the energy is specifically directed.

Follow the Natural

In Tai Chi and Chi Kung there is typically an emphasis on natural alignments and energy flow. Also, the breathing tends to be relaxed, slow, smooth, deep and comfortable like a sleeping infant child. The idea here is to achieve a state where many of the body's higher level energy functions will occur automatically at the same time without thought or effort on the part of the practitioner even though personal awareness has been increased. Deep relaxation without tension is highly desired. This is commonly referred to by serious internal practitioners as "Follow the Natural".

Urination and bowel movements are two natural body functions. The most common use of Yi in modern society is the conscious control over these functions. Delaying the elimination of waste and holding it in until the opportunity to go to a bathroom in a designated place becomes available and deciding when to let the waste go is a function of Yi. Usually there is no emotion surrounding the elimination of waste but there is the conscious decision or at least the awareness to hold it and when and where to let go. This delay and holding becomes such an automatic act that a lot of the time the average person is unaware that they are controlling this function and it falls slightly below the active conscious awareness. The only way this changes is if the person chooses to focus and become aware of it.

Consciously deciding to relax and then physically relaxing is also a function of Yi. Practicing to gain the mental control over this process will build your Yi. A simple exercise to practice this is to intentionally tense just your shoulders and then let go and let the shoulders fully drop and relax. You can repeat this same intentional tensing and relaxing process with almost any part of your body including the arms or legs and with a little bit of practice you can tense the whole body and then relax the whole body. The trick is to be aware enough of your entire body so that after you have relaxed there are no areas where you are still holding tension. This kind of relaxation that can be or is active while not holding any tension is called *Sung* in *Chinese* and is one of the primary physical requirements necessary for the development of the ability to work with energy. The mind gets as much or more out of this training than the body does.

The awareness to truly be able to feel the level of tension or relaxation in your entire body at any given moment is a true reflection of the development or lack thereof of your mind and the Yi and is one of the more important aspects of energy work development. Without proper attention being given to this aspect of energy work it will be very difficult to make any significant achievement or real progress in energy work.

QUIET THE MIND

Quieting the mind is one of the most important practices necessary to develop the mind. Listening to and/or feeling and following your own breath with your mind is a powerful and basic beginning way to train to get quiet and to learn how to use the Yi internally. The jing in this case is called Listening and is one of the most often overlooked and important jings there is. If you cannot sense energy and energy movement then it will be nearly impossible to control energy. Feeling and or being sensitive to the movement of ones own breath inside the body is an excellent way to begin to feel the movement of energy inside your body. Also, as an exercise, limited holding of the breath while physically relaxing will help build the Yi. The following two breath exercises as well as many of the other exercises in this book (particularly Wu Chi, 3 Dan Tiens Linear and Marrow Washing Breathing) will help you to begin to develop true inner quiet.

Breathe in. Then, hold the breath for 30 seconds or more while relaxing. This will help you feel and build the energy level in the body.

Breathe out. Then, hold the breath for 30 seconds or more while relaxing. This will help you feel and build the relaxed state of the body.

JING = ENERGY EXPRESSION

Energy can express or be expressed in many different ways. Jing is the Chinese term for Energy expression. Typically when the word Jing is used we are referring to it as an *expression* of Chi directed by the Mind Intent. Internal Kung Fu is a common way for people to describe arts that specifically focus on the utilization of Chi. However, for an art to really be internal the energy that is happening inside the body needs to be more than or at least as significant as what is happening outside the body. True "high level" internal power can be felt but cannot be seen unless the practitioner chooses to show it.

ADVANCED CHI KUNG WARNING

Most of the Chi Kung taught in this book is simple and designed to be easy to learn and to practice. However, it is good to follow common sense when practicing any Chi Kung. The warning that follows is very important for anyone who is seriously practicing Chi Kung and is an excellent rule of thumb for practicing the internal arts.

The idea in the internal arts and most Chi Kung is to change the body from the inside out and hence whatever you put into your body must be taken into consideration in this process. It is wise to be cautious particularly when practicing any exercise that is designed to move energy through the body and into or out of the core and/or the bone marrow of the body. Remember that DNA is a spiral shape which indicates movement along the length and breadth of the shape and from the outside to the inside and vice-versa.

1. <u>DO NOT USE alcohol or drugs</u> within 24 hours before or after practicing Chi Kung. These substances will become part of your body if you practice energy arts with them in your body. So, Keep the Body as clean as possible. (Alcohol and Nicotine are drugs.)
DO NOT SMOKE

2, Eat healthy and well balanced meals and consider natural vitamins or supplements as part of your overall diet plan. If need be consult a physician about this aspect of your health. Drink water and cut back on or eliminate unnatural liquids such as soda pop. It is fairly common for people who practice Chi Kung to develop higher sensitivity to tastes, smells and the body's natural reactions to toxic substances and unhealthy substances can become much more noticeable to the practitioner. When I first began seriously practicing I personally found that I could not eat certain meats for awhile as they tasted horrible to me.

3. Do not abuse your body. As you practice and gain energy from the practice of Chi Kung it is common to get an energy boost unlike any you may have felt before. This energy is best when conserved and used to have full healthy days and a long life.

4. Beware of extreme and excessive emotional states. They can rob you of energy. Extreme anger, fear or sadness can actually do a lot of physical harm to you. <u>Learn to pay attention to your emotions and why they are occurring because usually there is a</u> reason for them and if you address the issue(s) that cause the emotion then you have opened a door to peace and harmony while getting more enjoyment out of life.

5. If you are under age then please abstain from sex. If you are an unmarried adult then consider what is best and most healthy for you.

Many people think that sex must be abstained from for long periods of time when practicing Chi Kung. This is not true for most Chi Kung. However, do not abuse your body by practicing Chi Kung then having lots of sex then practicing some more Chi Kung. Sexual essence is made up of some of the most powerful chemicals in the body such as testosterone and proteins. These same chemicals are being utilized by the energy systems of the body when practicing Chi Kung. It is best to wait for at least 12 hours after sex to practice Chi Kung so that the body has had time to replenish itself. There are specific methods of practice to retain the sexual essence so that it is not lost during the sex act. Either ask your instructor or consult books written by Mantak Chia to learn specifically how to do this practice.

6. It is always best to learn Chi Kung from someone who is truly qualified. Make sure to stay in close contact with your instructor two to three times a week and report on how your practice is progressing and what you are experiencing from the Chi Kung practice.

7. Report any new, strange or unpleasant experiences or sensations to your instructor as soon as possible so that corrections and adjustments can be made if needed. Often the corrections are as simple as relax more here or breathe more easily or slight postural adjustments. Quite often with Chi Kung a little bit goes a long way and what may not seem like much at first eventually becomes a big deal.

8. Do not practice internal Power building or Energizing Chi Kung within 4 hours of sleep. So, if your bedtime is 10 p.m. then 6 p.m. should be the absolute latest time in the day that you practice this type of Chi Kung. There is specific relaxing and calming Chi Kung that can be practiced to help you calm down and go to sleep and this can be practiced later in the day.

9. Do not focus Chi into your head or heart without specific instruction and guidance from a certified instructor.

Proper Relaxation, Refined Body Alignments and Attention to Detail are all essential to real success in the Internal Arts.

ESSENTIAL TAI CHI

Tai Chi = Grand Ultimate Energy

Tai can be translated as Grand Ultimate. So, Tai Chi translates as Grand Ultimate Energy. The full name of this Internal Chi Kung based martial art in Chinese is Tai Chi Chuan. Chuan translates as fist. Hence the real translated name of the style is Grand Ultimate Energy Fist. Yang style is the most popular Tai Chi style taught in the world today. Most of the time in the West the art is taught as Tai Chi without the Chuan. Also, more often than not the moves and choreography that make up the basics of the system are taught in a tranquil and slow moving pattern of 24, 48, 88 or 108 moves. There are at least 4 popular styles of Tai Chi and there are many other styles of Tai Chi including Family styles, modified styles and styles from specific parts of the country such as Wu Tang Mountain (the area of China and monks referenced in the movie "Crouching Tiger Hidden Dragon"). In Clear's Modified Yang style Tai Chi there is an 8, 13, 18, 48 and 108 movement pattern available. Any of the sets will provide benefit as long as the energy and proper body mechanics are present.

In this text and in all of our Tai Chi programs we are interested in the Chi aspect of the Tai Chi and submit that the moves without the Activation and Cultivation of the Chi are simply choreography and are like a pretty car without any fuel or spark and hence although the car can be pushed around it is at an expense of energy as opposed to building energy. If the Chi was not important then slow ballroom dancing could be used to accomplish the same benefits. It is our purpose in this text to illustrate how to activate, build and circulate the energy for health and vitality.

Tai Chi is still being academically researched and studied in the West and has already been proven to help and provide relief for a broad range of health problems including but not limited to arthritis, hypertension, high blood pressure, migraines, Multiple Sclerosis, balance and immune system deficiencies. It is the Chi part of the Tai Chi being activated, built and circulated that has this effect. You can practice Chi Kung by itself. However, once you can activate the Chi and understand how the energy feels while it is being built, accumulated and circulated you can practice your Chi Kung while doing Tai Chi. Then, you can really begin to get the more remarkable effects that have caused Tai Chi to become well known as an excellent alternative healing practice. If you are already a student of Tai Chi then after practicing the Wu Chi and 3 Dan Tiens Linear practice (presented on page 38 and 77 in this book) for awhile try to do the Tai Chi with these same body mechanics and energies flowing. The movements are secondary to the energy. Once again, it is working with the Chi in Tai Chi that provides the majority of the publicized benefits.

Wu Chi

Wu Chi = <u>Energy is Activated</u> & No Physical <u>Movement</u>

Wu Chi builds and then circulates energy.

Wu in this connotation refers to no physical action while the Chi energy is still present. In Chinese an ideogram or picture is used to signify and convey meaning instead of an alphabet of 26 letters. There are thousands of these pictures and they can be combined in many different ways to produce very complex meanings within just a few symbols.

The first thing that proper Wu Chi practice will do is cause the body to activate the energy of the 3 Powers of Heaven, Earth and Man. Man takes in the energy of the earth and sky and changes or transmutes it into a form that can be used by man. The Yin Yang symbol  *heaven* signifies this by the light heaven energy and the dark earth energy contained *earth* within a boundary and mixing together. The 3 Powers was originally signified by a drawing of a cauldron with a fire below it and steam expressing from the top going skywards.

This is to illustrate the idea that physically man is a vessel made of mostly liquid that heats up when properly worked (the fire can be felt in the legs by beginners) and so the essence inside begins to act like steam and travel around the body.

In time the Wu Chi posture done correctly will cause the energy in the body to build and then to flow and circulate unrestricted first in the micro-cosmic orbit and then in the macro-cosmic orbit.

In Here

Micro-cosmic orbit

The micro-cosmic orbit also known as the small circulation is an energy circulation around the torso starting in the nose moving down the front of the body then underneath the torso to the bottom of the spine and moving up the center of the back and moving up and over the middle of the head then down the front of the face and down the middle of the front of the body again. In acupuncture terms the energy is moving through the Governing and Conception Vessel Meridians.

The Small Universe, also known as the small circulation or Microcosmic Obit, refers to the flow of vital chi energy around the body through the Ren Mai and Du Mai Meridians. The Ren or Conception Meridian runs from just below the lower lip down the front part of the body to just before the anus. The Du or Governing Meridian starts just after the anus and just before the tailbone and follows the spine in a straight line over the top of the head down the nose and ends between the nose and upper lip.

The macro-cosmic orbit also known as the Grand or large Circulation is the same as the micro-cosmic orbit except that in the macro-cosmic orbit the energy also flows around the entire body including the arms and legs. You will know when you have achieved this because you will feel the energy all over the body including in the feet and the feet may feel like they are sweating. Once you have achieved this focus on deeply relaxing and feeling the sensation over the entire body. Do Not over focus on the feet as this will cause the body to improperly overheat.

The idea is for the energy to circulate through these pathways and to gain speed and strength while widening/opening the meridians (energy lines in the body that Chi flows through) so that more Chi can flow. One of the many benefits of the Wu Chi posture is that it allows this process to happen automatically without any interference or conscious direction needed from the practitioner. If the practitioner mentally forces the process then there is the grave and likely possibility of accumulating too much mental and physical tension that will lead to great harm if not properly addressed. Allowing the relaxed body posture to accomplish these energy processes is the natural way and is much better.

<u>Wu Chi</u>

1. Hang From an Invisible Thread
2. Shoulders Hanging & Relaxed
3. All Joints Slightly Bent & Relaxed
4. Eyes Relaxed & Look Slightly Down
5. Relax & Drop Down Lower Back
6. Spine is Pulled Straight by Gravity
7. Point Index Fingers Straight
8. Breathe In & Out From Belly
9. Tongue Lightly Touches Roof of The Mouth Behind Front Teeth
10. Weight is slightly to the Front of Center over the Feet

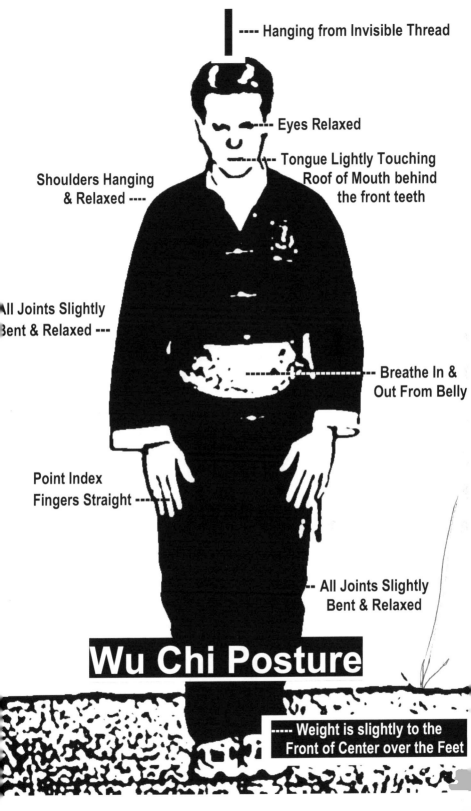

1. *Hang From an Invisible Thread*

Imagine that you are hanging from an invisible bungee cord that is lifting your body upwards and straightening your spine. The idea here is to feel buoyant like a ball floating on water and yet gravity is pulling your body weight down. The cord attaches at the top and back of your head directly above the spine. Every other part of your body is hanging. At first just stand this way and after you have practiced long enough that you can easily get into the feeling of this posture then see if you can walk around this way. Getting the feeling of the Invisible Thread is very healthy for the body as it aligns your posture and allows the energy to flow unrestricted.

2. Shoulders Hanging & Relaxed

Raise only your shoulders as high as you can so that you can feel the effort of holding them up. Then let the shoulders drop and relax as much as possible while breathing out to help to get the shoulders completely hanging and relaxed without tension. If you are really standing with the shoulders correctly relaxed and hanging then It should be easy to swing the arms a little just by swaying the body back and forth. Also, the arms may feel a little heavy.

3. All Joints Slightly Bent & Relaxed

A simple way to help get the right position for this is to stand up straight and rigid then let go and relax everywhere just enough so that no more excess tension is being held anywhere in the body. In other words it feels like you just relaxed every part of your body. Then sink a little and relax again the same way about another quarter to half inch everywhere. This should put you into the correct posture.

4. Eyes Relaxed & Look Slightly Down

The eyes are about half way between open and closed and very relaxed while looking slightly down as in the diagram. This helps to conserve energy and it actually increases the field of vision and helps make it easier to quickly perceive motion.

5. *Relax & Drop Down Lower Back*

The ideal situation is to have the lower back drop so that there is no bend between the middle of the back and the bottom of the buttocks. This often takes work on the part of the beginner to get it right and may well require the assistance of another person. It is possible to help develop this posture by stepping back against the wall so that the back of your heels are against the wall and placing your back flat against the wall and trying to get your entire back from the middle of your shoulders to the bottom of the buttocks on the wall. After this can be

done with comfort then step away
from the wall and maintain the flat
back position.

6.   Spine is Pulled Straight by Gravity

Strive to keep your body weight under you and pulling down by keeping the head pulling up as if it is being pulled up by a bungee cord and the body is relaxed and the weight of the body is relaxed and dropping so that you feel the weight of your body as if hanging from the bungee cord.

7.   Point Index Fingers Straight

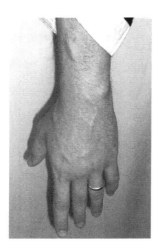 Point the index finger while staying relaxed and keep the rest of the fingers relaxed and not bent but not particularly straight either.

8. *Breathe In & Out From Belly*

The beginning way to breathe is to breathe in and out from the belly. This may be a little difficult at first but it will become much easier with practice. If you have never practiced belly breathing before it may be easier to learn to belly breathe by practicing the following exercise by itself first. Push into your belly with your fingers. When you breathe in use the air to push the belly out and move your fingers out of your belly with the air.

BELLY BREATHE ALL THE TIME

Teach yourself to belly breathe until it is the natural way you breathe without having to consciously think about it. This means do it as much as possible all of the time. Babies naturally breathe this way and most people breathe this way when they sleep because the body is at its most relaxed and utilizes the deep and steady oxygenation to recharge the body. This is the natural and healthy way to breathe. Really try it for 30 days and see how different you feel. Not only will you have more energy when you belly breathe but your stress level will actually decrease as well.

Many people in modern society breathe high up towards the top part of the lungs and have difficulty getting good quality deep full breaths. This is a direct result of the stress and tension that most people carry with them in modern day life. As people and animals get close to dying they breathe higher and higher in the body until the last few breaths are so high up in the body that they tend to be rapid and shallow and actually occur in the throat.

Also, when most people run or jog for any length of time they end up gasping for air. It is because the body is depleted of oxygen and is demanding more. Why wait until you are out of air to really breathe? That is like waiting until you are completely dehydrated to drink water.

I have learned a substantial amount of my Kung Fu, Tai Chi and Chi Kung from Si-Tai-Gung Tyrone Jackson. I became a Sifu and eventually a Sigung under his tutelage. He was the senior disciple under Dr. Fred Wu. Dr Wu was the senior master of my primary Kung Fu and Chi Kung systems. Dr Wu lived to be over 100 years old. He once told my father and I, when no one else was around, that belly breathing is one of the real Chinese Secrets to health and longevity. After over 30 years of studying and practicing the arts from many different systems all over the world I can safely say that he was right. I think now I will take a deep breath!

9. Tongue Lightly Touches Roof of The Mouth Behind the Front Teeth

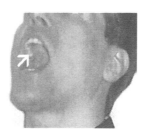

The tongue lightly touches the roof of the mouth behind the front teeth while keeping your mouth closed. Lightly means let the tongue rest there while keeping the mouth closed and breathe in and out through your nose. This will connect the energy circuit between the Ren Mai and Du Mai Governing and Conception Vessel meridians causing the energy to flow without interruption. One of the first effects you may notice from this is that you will have more stamina.

10. *Weight is slightly to the Front of Center over the Feet*

You do not have to bend and drop into an uncomfortable position while you practice standing in Wu Chi. You can actually stand up tall while you are practicing as you only need a few inches of drop. The biggest trick is to unlock your legs and let the rest of the body fully relax to the same extent. This is true for most of the standing Chi Kung presented in this book.

ENERGY ACTIVATION

Wu Chi activates the energy and then builds and circulates it. When practicing Wu Chi beginners may feel any number of sensations including but not limited to hot, cold, electricity, the micro or macro cosmic energy circuit or magnetic sensations. Work with Wu Chi until you can feel the slight sensation of electricity or heat or until the veins on your hands look full when you look at them like the example picture included here.

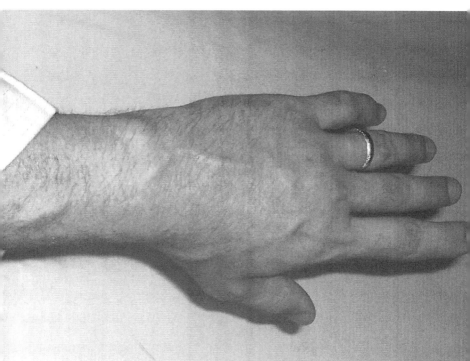

THE ENERGY BALL

Stand in the Wu Chi posture. Then, while staying relaxed and continuing to circulate the energy of the Wu Chi posture slowly take your hands and place them about 3-5 inches apart and feel for the sensation between your hands.

(See Picture: Holding the Energy Ball)

Stay relaxed and hold the posture and see how the feeling between your hands changes and grows. With a little practice you will be able to get into the Wu Chi posture and feel the activation of the energy this way almost immediately. With a little more practice your hands will generate a warm, electrical and/or magnetic energy that most people will describe as a feeling of heat from several inches away. Holding the Energy Ball is a simple way to check the energy flow of your Wu Chi Posture. At this stage it is not important what others feel but it is very important what you feel.

Holding the Energy Ball

Rooting & Sinking

Drop as much of the body weight as possible down into the soles of the feet so that the rest of the body feels light. Hanging from the invisible thread will help with this. Relaxing, letting go and melting every tension out of the body down into the ground so that the feet contain all of the body weight is also a good practice and a good way to get this happening. When this is done correctly any movement from either foot will be expressed by the entire body.

For higher level rooting/sinking skill "Invest in Loss" and allow yourself to let go. Practice standing and letting your energy sink into the ground through the Yong Quan empty hollow in the middle of the bottom of the feet (see illustration page 86). You are not practicing to lose energy doing this but instead are staying connected and seeking to gain depth and energetic strength through letting your energy travel by letting it go the easiest and most natural direction possible which is downwards with the force of gravity.

BODY CONNECTION

One of the goals of Wu Chi and Rooting and sinking is to build body connection. With proper practice of Wu Chi and Rooting and sinking you will begin to build body connection. Body connection is important because it allows the chi energy to flow unimpeded around the body and it builds the foundation for high level internal body quality and health. If you use electricity as a model then picture the physical body as being similar in nature to an electrical wire that the electricity flows through and around. The body is a conductor of bio-electro-magnetic energy. The problem is that with modern day living most people have allowed their wires to get broken or to get clogged up and so the energy will not flow correctly. A water hose analogy might work as a better visual model for this. If the hose has a kink in it the water will not flow through it very well and sometimes not at all. Mental and physical tension, injuries and poor physical care of the body through poor posture and/or diet have put many kinks in the average person's hose/body.

In his book "The Body Electric" Robert O. Becker, M.D., a pioneer in the field of bioelectric science, presents a fascinating look at the role electricity plays in healing through his research, and breakthrough discoveries. He used artificial (non-organic) low level electrical stimulation for his studies and stimulated patient's injuries with electrical treatments and documented the powerful results of increased and faster healing because of the electrical stimulation. This is truly a great body of work because it proves what the Chinese having been practicing with their own bodies for over a thousand years. The difference is that God gave us the ability to heal ourselves and that power exists within our own bodies. The trick is getting the electricity to flow unimpeded. This is where body connection comes in. Also, our body is designed to flow the correct voltage and amount of electricity to do the most efficient healing job possible.

BUOYANCY = ROOTING AND FLOATING

When practicing Wu Chi or/and Rooting and Sinking a simple way to tell if you have Body Connection is that you should feel buoyant like a fishing bobber floating on top of the water with the waist and below feeling like it is under the water while from the waist up feels light and easily movable. To be specific the legs from the thighs down should feel like they are being crushed by the weight of the entire body all being in them and the body from the waist up should feel like it is light as a feather and floating on top of the midsection. This is again the body expressing the 3 powers of Tai Chi and part of the reason for the symbol ☯. The dark part of the symbol is the heavy legs. The light part of the symbol is the upper body and the dots are the little bit of each that are in the other. The dividing line is the midsection and where the 2 are mixed. Done properly this Body Connection allows the energy to flow unimpeded through the body. The trick is to allow it to flow and not to allow yourself to become tense or to hold tension in an area and also not to try to cheat the position. If you are not dropping the weight then body connection is not happening. Wu Chi is not as difficult to do at first because the legs are together and the stance is higher.

Usually beginners will still feel it after a little while however and will need to be careful not to overdue it or they may become discouraged by the resulting sore legs and thighs that occur for the next day or two after practice. The good news is that with a little bit of time the leg strength will grow and the benefits of the practice will make it worth the minor inconvenience at the beginning.

This practice will eventually make the body very strong and resistant to illness. Along with rooting it is also the beginning of Iron Body training, a Chi Kung practice of making the body very resiliently strong so that it can withstand very hard blows. Some of this is the result of the energy accumulation and circulation and part of it is due to specific practice methods that build the body's internal ligaments, tendons and muscle viscera which is the tissue between the organs and muscles. Specific practices for developing Iron Body are taught in each of our programs and are specific to the particular style or method and the age and physical constitution of the individual practitioner.

REMOVING BLOCKAGES

The desired physical state In Traditional Chinese medicine (TCM) is for balance and for the energy to flow anywhere and everywhere throughout the body without impediment. From a physical standpoint energy blockages are seen as one of the main barriers to this process. The removal of blockages is a significant subject of study in TCM. Blockages can occur due to injuries, illness and even through physical, mental or spiritual stress and/or tension. An area becomes damaged or is tensed/injured for long enough that energy becomes backed up behind the blocked area and the energy is unable to flow around the blocked area or the energy flows around the blockage typically creating an area in which a more localized but quite often expanding energy block occurs. From a Chi Kung standpoint there are a number of ways to deal with such blockages. A great deal of simple energy blockages can be removed through stretching and working (flexing and massaging etc) any area that is affected to simply breathing and relaxing through and around the affected area. Of course the idea is to practice so that energy blockages either don't happen in the first place or to get to the point in training where undue stress and tension are immediately noticed and handled so that an energy blockage does not form and can not gain a foothold on/in the body. Along with the following exercise all of the practices in the next chapter help to facilitate body alignment and remove and stop the formation of energy blockages.

Body Relaxing Practice

Relax your entire body one step at a time. Start from the top of your head and work your way down to your toes. Isolate each body part as you do the work. So, relax the top of your head first then progress to your face and relax the forehead, eyes and cheeks etcetera. Then move your attention down to your neck starting with the area under the chin and so on and so forth until you get all the way to the bottom of the feet. Try to feel as if you are melting. Do not skip areas and really take your time. If need be relax inch by inch so that you do not miss an area. If you make this practice a regular habit then it will become much easier and you will get faster at it. You will become much better at noticing tensions and blockages attempting to form in the body and you will begin to get a lot better at circumventing physical stress before it can become a long term part of your body and movement. In fact after several weeks of practice you will most likely not allow inappropriate and unnecessary tension to stay in your body for very long because you will find it uncomfortable and you will notice how much energy it drains form you and how long term unhealthy it is. All of this benefit will primarily be derived from what and how you feel which makes it a practice that becomes a part of you and you will begin to automatically maintain this state after awhile. This is a lot of benefit to gain from such an easy and simple practice.

If you are having a problem relaxing an area or finding the tension then there are a number of tricks to help sort this out. One method is to tense the area as much as possible, hold it and then allow the area to fully relax as much as possible. You can also breathe in to the area while tensing it and then hold the breath while holding the tension. When relaxing let the tension go and let the tension drain out with the breath.

Eventually you will be able to immediately draw tension out of your body by pulling it with your breath, holding it for a moment then sending it out with your breath. Try drawing out a headache with your breath the next time you feel one coming on.

ENERGY ALIGNMENT

Proper energy alignment will make it much easier to root and gain strong body connection. Following are three practices that will help to facilitate this process. They are Body Bouncing, Brushing and Patting. Body Bouncing settles, roots and aligns the Chi while Brushing and Patting leads the Chi into root and alignment.

Body Bouncing

Stand in Wu Chi and relax downwards about another inch. Now, gently bounce up and down as if standing on a flexible surface such as a trampoline. Your feet don't show the movement. Let the vibration from the bounce go through every part of your body particularly your internal organs, arms and legs. Your arms may swing. Be gentle on the amount of bounce you allow your head to feel. Do this practice for several minutes at a time.

Brushing to Align the Chi

Start from the top of your head and gently brush (downwards only) with short swipes as if brushing off lint. Work your way down your neck, arms, torso and legs until finally you wipe off your toes. Each time you go for another swipe your hand should start lower on your body than where you started the last swipe and it should also finish lower than end of the last swipe.

Patting to Lead and Seal the Chi

Pat down your body by heavily dropping your hands. Start at your upper arms and shoulders and only pat downwards as in Brushing until you pat the tops of your feet.

STORING AND BALANCING ENERGY

Storing and balancing Chi Energy is an important and not commonly understood aspect of Chi Kung practice. Essentially, the process is as follows. Energy is gathered, accumulated and activated. Then, energy is circulated and Chi Kung to facilitate better and more activation and circulation may be practiced. These practices tend to refine the quality of the Chi and allow the physical body to better accumulate and hold more energy. The next step is to balance and store the Chi so that the amount of quality energy stored in the body may be increased and utilized for health and other uses. It is exceptionally important to balance and store the Chi after circulating it so that it does not disperse or cause the practitioner to look for external and generally energy destroying ways to calm the energy down.

My Chinese teachers have referred to storing Chi in the following manner. "Storing Chi is like putting money in the bank. I want to store as much as possible and collect interest so that I will truly be wealthy in my old age." Having Chi attracts more Chi similar to the way that electricity conducts and electrifies what it comes into contact with and the way that magnets magnetize nearby metal.

Balancing the Chi means to settle the Chi and to bring it to a state that is good for the body hence not to hot or cold or to light or heavy and not stagnant but not hyperactive. In fact, a calm and steady relaxed Wu Chi type state where the entire body and/or Chi is tranquil but can be easily mobilized or utilized as a unit is most desired.

Two of the most important practices for balancing and storing energy are the "Carry the Cauldron" and "Grand Tai Chi" exercises. Three correctly performed Carry the Cauldron exercises will balance the back Meridians. Three proper Grand Tai Chi exercises will balance the Meridians in the front of the body. Both of the exercises settle the Chi and if they are practiced together then the exercises will balance and correct the entire meridian and energy system. Carry the Cauldron utilizes a special breathing method and refines the energy and Grand Tai Chi settles and stores the Chi. So, these are the last two exercises to practice after finishing most other types of Chi Kung.

If you finish practicing any kind of Chi Kung or have experienced an *energy disturbance* of some kind and are concerned that you may have incorrectly practiced and/or there is an *energy blockage* or intention has been misplaced or any other kind of *energetic imbalance* has occurred then practice at least three or more repetitions of Carry the Cauldron and then the same number of repetitions of Grand Tai Chi to fix the *energetic* problem. (E*nergetic* problems NOT physical ones! DO NOT start performing these exercises if you have physically overdone it or have strained your back or need to rest.) To correct an energetic problem may require more than three repetitions of each exercise if the problem is severe enough or you are having a difficult time properly performing or moving energy with these two exercises. Fortunately, you can do as many repetitions of this Chi Kung as you want or need with no *energetic* harm and *energetically* no ill after effects.

If you are trying to fix a longer term health or energetic problem then you may want to start a daily practice of these two exercises along with other health care treatment including but not limited to visiting a TCM doctor and regular Western physicians for diagnosis and treatment along with any and all necessary follow up. Tell them about these exercises and get their release and permission prior to continuing to practice.

Carry the Cauldron

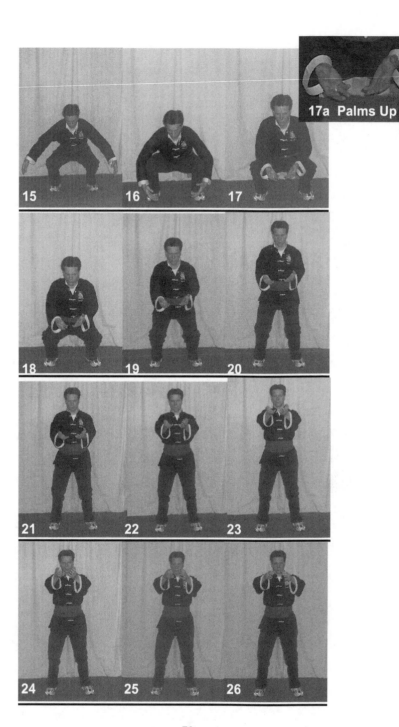

17a Palms Up

Continually repeat the exercise from photos # 13 – 34 without interruption or finish the form as in pictures 35 & 36 here ➔

Carry the Cauldron
Instructions

Photos 1 – 4   Breathe in and lift your hands so that you can see both of your palms. Carry the Cauldron is performed in one continuous movement.

Photos 5 & 6   Turn your palms so that they face out in front of you and you can no longer see them.
Slowly begin breathing out.
Match the breath speed to the movement.

Photos 7 – 10   Turn your palms so that they are facing out to the sides and move the arms out until you feel like you are gently pushing against a wall with each hand. Continue slowly breathing out.

Photos 11 – 14   Bend your knees and drop your arms while continually pushing out against the invisible walls with each palm. Continue slowly breathing out. Stay Relaxed.

Photos 15 – 24	Begin breathing in. The breath should be slow, smooth, deep, and comfortable.
	Imagine picking up a large and heavy black kettle/cauldron like in the original KUNG FU television series. Continue breathing in and Lift it up as high as you can by holding it with your palms and forearms.
Photos 25 – 27	Drop the Kettle and breathe out as if dropping a heavy weight.
Photos 28 – 34	Repeat Photo moves 5-27 as much as needed or desired.
Photos 35 & 36	When you are ready to finish then let the arms drop back to the sides and step back into the Wu Chi position. Breathe in. Then breathe out and fully relax and let your root drop down through your body and into the ground.

Grand Tai Chi

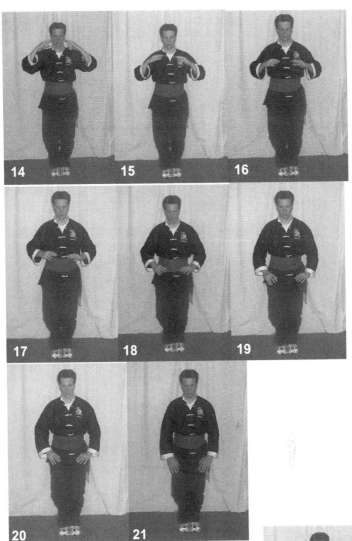

Continually repeat the
exercise from photos # 4 –
21 without interruption or
finish the form as in picture
22 included here ➔

Grand Tai Chi
Instructions

1. Begin by Standing in Wu Chi.

2. Breathe in as you lift your hands and feel yourself scoop the energy up into your cupped palms. The breath should be slow, smooth, deep and comfortable.

3. Once your hands get as high as they can go then turn your open palms over towards your head and drop the energy into your Bai Hui.

4. Slowly breathe out and let the energy settle and drop through you. Do not push or force the energy down in any way. Let Gravity do the work.

5. IMPORTANT: Drop your hands down in front of you *slower* than the energy is dropping inside of you. You may feel that your hands are floating on top of the energy. This is good.

6. Continually repeat the cycle of movement and breathing until you are ready to stop. When you are ready to stop then drop your hands back to your sides and continue to do Wu Chi.

3 DAN TIENS LINEAR

The primary physical idea in 3 Dan Tiens Linear is to line up the Upper, Middle and Lower Dan Tien vertically as if they are pearls hanging on a string. This makes the Chi flow powerfully and there is a lot of very impressive health benefits to just getting and holding this alignment position for awhile. Once you have accomplished the proper alignment you will know because it will make you feel very calm, comfortable, centered and connected to everything around you as if you are a part of the surroundings. It is a very pleasant feeling (although to many it will probably seem strange at first) and it is most correct when you find that your mind is very quiet and that all your worries and troubles melt away as this is a very stress relieving Chi Kung that makes you temporarily forget almost everything. As with most stress reducing activities this type of Chi Kung can help you to recover quickly from fatigue.

This Chi Kung will automatically open your small and large circulations to Chi and the chi will automatically circulate without requiring any conscious direction. This combined with the mind calming and stress relieving benefits make it so that even if you are extremely tired you can completely recover after practicing this Chi Kung for about 15 minutes. To reap the higher level health benefits I always recommend that you get a good night of sleep and then utilize the Chi Kung practices to enhance and complement your state of physical and mental health. I recommend that when you first learn this Chi Kung you should practice while standing. After you have practiced for a while and can easily get into and perform the 3 Dan Tiens Linear then you can begin to practice while sitting, laying down, walking or practicing Tai Chi. This Chi Kung does not require any preparation or special procedure before stopping. However, I highly recommend that you perform the Carry the Cauldron and Grand Tai Chi exercise once you have completed your practice of 3 Dan Tiens Linear.

<u>DO NOT Practice this Chi Kung while driving or operating any kind of machinery</u> etc as you will most likely not notice or pay attention to your surroundings resulting in a terrible and horrendous accident!

<u>3 DAN TIENS LINEAR VISUALIZATION METHOD</u>

1. Start by performing Wu Chi.

2. Find and feel the Upper Dan Tien and then immediately find, feel and concentrate on the Lower Dan Tien. Be attentive to the feeling of Chi in the Lower Dan Tien.

3. Picture a plumb line dropped from the Upper Dan Tien that falls vertically through the position of the Lower Dan Tien and the Lower Dan Tien is

attached to the line like a pearl on a thread or a sinker on a fishing line.

4. Then, make slight movements of the body including slight movement of the upper torso, neck and head make small adjustments to the position of the line so that the line passes through the Middle Dan Tien and the Middle Dan Tien is also attached to the line. Do this gently and do not put any stress or pressure on the Middle Dan Tien.

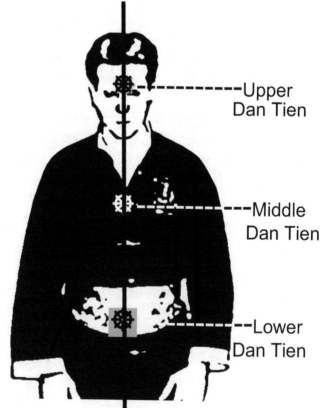

Upper
Dan Tien

Middle
Dan Tien

Lower
Dan Tien

5. To help make the 3 Dan Tiens vertically linear imagine each of the 3 Dan Tiens are spheres. The sphere of the middle Dan Tien should be carefully put between the sphere of the upper and lower Dan Tien. The middle sphere may be somewhat elusive if you are careless or not used to making the small adjustments necessary to get the proper alignment. Do not be in a hurry or try to force the position. A little patience and relaxation will go a long way.

6. Once you have accomplished the proper alignment you will know because it will make you feel very calm, comfortable, centered and connected to everything around you as if you are a part of the surroundings. Maintain this feeling for as long as possible. This special feeling/body mind state is said to help return you to your original balanced state that cures or alleviates the symptoms of diseases and promotes extraordinary health.

7. At the end of practicing 3 Dan Tiens Linear always remember to move the

Chi back down to the Lower Dan Tien or for more advanced practitioners back down the legs to be stored in the bone marrow in the legs. The easiest way to do this is to perform the Carry the Cauldron and the Grand Tai Chi (Chi Kung exercises on pages 69-76).

8. You should feel good and comfortable and not be tired after each practice. Start a little bit at a time and gradually increase the duration of each session. Do not be in a hurry. Rome was not built in a day. Do not over practice as over practice will tend to take away more benefit than it will give.

9. Mastering the duration and degree of internal heat is an important problem when practicing Chi Kung. If you begin to experience Xerostomia (dry mouth due to a lack of saliva) then you may be over practicing and need to shorten your practice sessions for now. If you begin to suffer from Xerostomia for other reasons such as to much focus on the Yong Quan (the hollow in the middle of the bottoms of the feet) which can happen because your mind is

drawn to the sensation of heat in the feet then change your focus and concentrate on the Mingmen a point in the middle of the hollow area on the small of the back and the problem should go away (see diagram page 87).

10. There is some disagreement amongst various Chi Kung Masters and TCM practitioners about point locations and designations. The points I have listed here are shown as I have learned and practiced them over many years. However, in all fairness I believe it is worthwhile in this instance to present other opinions/possible options on the subject. I have seen the Upper Dan Tien presented as Bai Hui and as another point separate from the 3rd eye position that I have been taught. I have seen the Lower Dan Tien presented as the Hui Yin and as the intersection between the two yong quan points with the intersection being somewhere between the feet depending on the posture. All of these points have in common that they are on the center line of the body and so may be helpful to students attempting to learn how to

perform this Chi Kung so I have included them here in order to provide as much assistance as possible in a manuscript of this type.

Another way to get the effect of 3 Dan Tiens Linear is to do Wu Chi and visualize that the thread/bungee cord you are hanging from enters your Bai Hui, continues down through your body and exits through your Hui Yin in a straight line and continues down into the ground. You should actually feel and not just imagine the alignment of the straight line. Now, imagine that there is a weight hanging at the bottom of the thread/line and that the weight pulls the line straight. The trick here is to feel the weight enough so that you will maintain the straightest body alignment possible and stay very relaxed while you are doing it. Done properly with relaxation this will greatly aid you in moving from and with your center because every time you move improperly off of center you will feel the weight at the bottom pulling you over.

High Level Practice

Mastering the Mind is the first step of real high level practice. The special mind and body state of 3 Dan Tiens Linear is very helpful for curing or alleviating the symptoms of diseases and promoting health. Once you have practiced long enough you will be able to enter this state just by thinking about it and it will be easy to practice 3 Dan Tiens Linear as part of your daily routine while doing other simple activities. **(I Repeat: DO NOT Drive, Operate heavy machinery or perform other potentially dangerous activities while doing this Chi Kung.)**

IMPORTANT POINTS

1. Bai Hui   2. Upper Dan Tien   3. Lao Gong
4. Middle Dan Tien   5. Lower Dan Tlen
6. Hui Yin   7. Yong Quan   8. Daz Hui   9. Mingmen

POINT NAMES & LOCATIONS

1. Bai Hui

The Bai Hui is on top and a little towards the back of the center of the head between the ears directly above the hypothalamus.

Bai Hui means 100 Meeting Places or 100 Convergences. It is Governing Vessel 20 (GV20) and is where the six yang channels converge and where heaven energy typically enters the body.

2. Upper Dan Tien

The Upper Dan Tien is between the eye brows and is also known as the third eye.

The Upper Dan Tien is considered a mental and spiritual psychic energy center. Dan Tien means Elixir Field or Energy Reservoir. Dan Tiens are bigger in size than regular pressure points.

3. Lao Gong

The Lao Gong is Pericardium 8 (PC8) and is located on the palm between the bones of the index and middle finger.

Lao Gong means Palace of Work. Properly flexing and exercising this area encourages the energy flow of the three yin and three yang channels found on the hand and expands the size of this energy center. It is one of the primary Gateways that Chi Kung practitioners use for sensing, conducting and directing energy.

4. Middle Dan Tien

The Middle Dan Tien is the Emotional Mind Center in the middle of the chest. It is considered to be the house of Shen because it contains the Chi that is created and directed by emotion and compassion. It makes sense that the Middle Dan Tien is located in the area we normally associate with our heart.

5. Lower Dan Tien

The Lower Dan Tien is the Physical strength and balance center. It is located 1-3 inches below the belly button. The Lower Dan Tien is traditionally considered to be the primary location where Chi is stored and is the area that is most commonly referred to and meant by the words Dan Tien when no other designation (such as upper, middle or lower) is given.

6. Hui Yin

The Hui Yin is Conception Vessel 1 (CV1). It means The Meeting of Yin. It is the meeting point on the Conception Vessel with the Governing and Penetrating/ Thrusting Vessels. The Hui Yin is located on the perineum in the center of the body directly between the anus and the genitals.

7. Yong Quan

Yong Quan is the hollow spot in the middle of the bottoms of the feet. It is the first point (KI 1) on the Kidney Meridian. Yong Quan means Bubbling Well and is called that because it is considered the beginning point where Chi flows into the body, Meridians and bones of the body.

8. Daz Hui

The Governing Vessel 14 (GV14) means Great Hammer. It is the meeting point on the Governing Vessel with the six yang channels. Also called the Sea of Qi Point, it is where the muscles, tendons and energy from the back and shoulders come together with the muscles, tendons and energy from the neck and head.

9. Mingmen

The Ming Men Governing Vessel 4 **(GV4)** is located in the lower back, between the second and third lumbar vertebra in what is usually thought of as the small of the back. Ming Men can be translated as the Gate of Destiny, Gate of Vitality or the Gate of Life. It is the true separation point between the upper and lower body and is the place where yin and yang and water (Kan) and fire (Li) meet in the body. This point regulates the higher level flow and mixture of energy in the body. Some consider it to be the beginning of the flow of energy through the energy system because this point controls the fire that is the source of personal willpower originating from the kidneys.

Bone Marrow Washing

Eternal Youth
Storing Energy to build up a surplus.

The Chi Follows the Mind

The biggest and most famous benefit of Bone Marrow Washing is the youth effect that it creates. Bone Marrow Washing is a deep breathing and visualization practice to help you breathe deeply and fill your body with healthy oxygenated breath and to help you to feel your entire body from the inside out such that over time it will rejuvenate the body from the deepest part inside the bone marrow. To put it simply, The Chi Follows the Mind. Get your mind to feel inside your bone marrow and the Chi will follow.

After several months of correct daily practice you will begin to notice that your bones have become more pliable and flexible like a child. This is partly because the microscopic holes in the skeletal bones, that close up in old age and cause the bones to become brittle, will open up again as the bone marrow expands and begins producing more healthy blood flow in the body. This practice builds up a surplus of stored Chi Energy in the bones and is commonly thought of by many Chi Kung masters/physicians as stored Jing. This helps to balance and settle the overall body Energy as well.

There are different ways to practice Bone Marrow Washing and there have been several books in English printed on this topic. I believe that the method I am presenting in this book is the safest and easiest direct method of acquiring this skill or Kung/Gong. I have seen methods that range from quite esoteric and difficult to understand to the exceptionally bizarre and weird. Frankly, I am not sure why this method has been kept such a high level secret because it is primarily a health method and can not really be misused to hurt others without very specific training for that purpose so the idea that the secret is kept to stop people from misusing it and hurting others does not really apply to this particular skill.

After you have first "mastered" belly breathing a more advanced way to breathe is into the nose and down through the body and legs into the feet and then releasing back up from the feet and back out through the nose while maintaining a high level of relaxation the entire time.

Many publicly available chi kung systems teach students to store energy in the lower dan tien. However, the secret inner school way is to store the energy using the idea that the whole body is like a battery and the bone marrow holds the charge and the legs are the largest repository of bone marrow in the body so most of the charge will store there. The primary step to doing this properly is to breathe in and out from the feet. Part of the breathing in and out to the depths of the feet is to help the practitioner to train their mind to feel to the farthest reaches of the extremities (fingers and toes) and eventually beyond.

Do not use this practice as a sleep replacement because then the real health effects will not manifest because you are using the energy up as you get it. Now having stated this, 20 minutes of proper Bone Marrow Washing is worth about 4 hours of sleep. Ideally, this energy is used to achieve a state of amazing health and vitality that improves your day to day life in new and meaningful ways because of how great you feel. I wish good health to you.

BONE MARROW BREATHING

1. Lay down on your back and place your hands at your side with your palms facing down.

2. Cross your legs so that your legs are crossed at the ankles. (See Picture page 96) Men cross left on top of right

and women cross right leg on top of the left. An easy way to remember this is that women are always right.

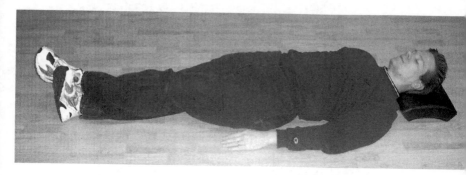

3.   **NOW RELAX.**   Relaxing is the most important part of this exercise.   The only way that this exercise can become harmful is if it is practiced improperly with tension or stress. So, relaxation is key.

4.   If anything about the Marrow Washing laying down position is uncomfortable then change the surface you are laying on or and take your hands off of the floor and lay them on your belly. You can do Marrow Washing while laying on a bed and/or with a pillow under your head.

Do not practice this method of Marrow Washing with the bottoms of your feet pointing at another person.

5. Relax some more and do some self talk to calm yourself down even more. Say "R-E-L-A-X" slowly, calmly and quietly to yourself and tell yourself that it is good to relax now and that you are feeling very relaxed (Said as "I am feeling very relaxed"). Take a deep breath and tense the body and hold it then let the breath out and let the tension go with it until you feel like you are melting into the floor or whatever surface you are laying on. Picture yourself melting and all tensions sinking away from you until they are all really truly gone.

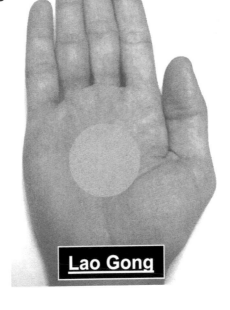

Lao Gong

6.   When you are completely relaxed begin breathing in through the hollow in the middle of the palms. Picture the energy you are breathing in as being earth energy from the ground. This spot is called Lao Gong in Chinese. Breathe in through the Lao Gong and visualize the air coming up the arms and down through the body to fill the belly.

At the same time, gently breathe in through the spot between your eyes known in the West as the 3rd Eye and as the Upper Dan Tien in Chinese Medicine. Breathe in heaven energy through this point and gently pull it down to the belly.

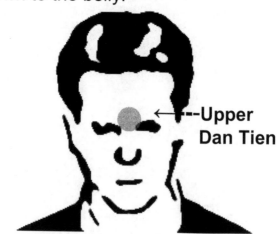

←--Upper
Dan Tien

Both the energy/breath from the Lao Gong and the energy/breath from the

Upper Dan Tien are pulled to and fill the belly at the same time. This gentle pull originates in the belly and pulls from the Lao Gong and Upper Dan Tien. The most important and biggest trick is to stay relaxed while doing this.

7. As you breathe in your belly will begin to accumulate some air in it. Do not force the accumulation or continue to breathe in past a point of comfort. In other words, you want to stop breathing in the second <u>before</u> there is even a hint of discomfort. This does not mean you will hold the breath. It simply means that once there is enough air in the belly you will begin the next step in the process.

8. Now, as you quit gently pulling in the air/energy with the stomach relax the belly and the whole abdominal area and also relax the whole body some more. While doing this, release the stored up air from the belly and let it flow down through the middle of your legs and down and out of the hollow spot in the middle of the bottoms of the feet. You want the energy to flow through the

legs like an ocean wave rolling into the shore.

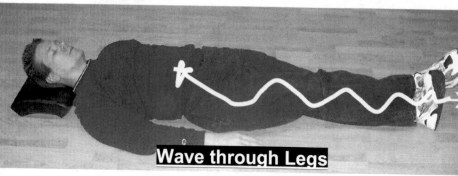

Wave through Legs

Let it go slowly. Do not try to speed up or push the energy down the legs.

The hollow spot in the middle of the bottoms of the feet is called the Yong Quan or Bubbling Well. This point is designated as Kidney 1 on the Kidney Meridian.

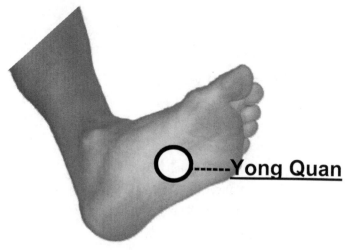

O------**Yong Quan**

9. Repeat steps 6 – 8 so that you are continually breathing this way. You can do this for as short a time as a few minutes or continue for as long as you want including sleeping through the night. There is no harm to you if you fall asleep doing this exercise and in fact it is beneficial if you intentionally fall asleep this way or use it to charge up first thing in the morning. Your mind will go into a deep state of relaxation like deep sleep when practicing this exercise. So, determine how long you want to do this practice before you begin so that you have a plan for when and how you are going to stop (ie an alarm or someone calling your name to wake you). My students have reported to me that when they are too excited and or cannot make themselves rest due to insomnia etc this method helps them go to sleep very quickly and enables them to get a really good night's rest.

10. When you quit doing the exercise and/or wake up slowly turn over and use your arms to lift yourself up. Massage your head and face including

scalp, eyes, ears and back of your neck slowly and firmly. Then, take a look around and *slowly* get up.

Do not jump right up to your feet. If you do you may injure yourself falling back down!

11. It is okay to practice Bone Marrow Washing with your feet facing a plant and imagine that you are exchanging good energy with the plant in the same manner that plants emit oxygen that we breathe and we emit carbon dioxide that plants breathe.

EMBRACE THE TREE
(HOLD THE BOWL)

The Embrace the Tree/Hold the Bowl Chi Kung is great for building the physical constitution, strengthening the legs, deep relaxation and increased internal Chi. It will build some other nice health benefits including Iron Shirt if practiced properly and consistently over an extended period of time (6 months or longer). I tend to refer to it as the aspirin of Chi Kung because it does a little bit of everything.

Embrace the Tree Posture

To properly perform the Embrace the Tree/Hold the Bowl posture it is recommended that you first do the Wu Chi standing posture with the proper energy and Body Connection. Then, move your feet so that you are standing with them about shoulder width apart and bend the knees a little bit more. While standing this way and maintaining the Wu Chi electrical energy feel slowly raise your arms to just above stomach height. Make your arms as round and relaxed as you can (as if holding a large ball) and keep the back straight as in the exercise standing up against the wall (on page 44). Learn to relax and use just enough strength to maintain the posture and be as relaxed and calm as possible. Also, feel the energy connect between the fingers of your left and right hand. Thumb connected to thumb, index to index and little finger to little finger.

Once you feel the energy connection if you hold your hands in front of a black background and continue to practice sleepy eye then you may be able to see the white energy between your fingers/hands. To learn more about

Embrace the tree and Iron Shirt see Mantak Chia's book on Iron Shirt I.

MORE ADVANCED PRACTICE

Hold the Ball with all of the Wu Chi principles in place and then add the energy of the energy ball, rooting, sinking, floating buoyancy, body connection and breathing deep and comfortably to/from the feet. Once this has been accomplished then try to practice Embrace the Tree and 3 Dan Tiens Linear at the same time.

FOR WOMEN ONLY

Women can start practicing Embrace the Tree/Hold the Bowl at 1-2 minutes per session and build to 5-6 minutes per session once or twice a day. Do not practice this while you are menstruating as it will jazz you up to much/make you jittery or/and agitated and you will not sleep well and possibly will not be able to sleep at all.

Within 3-4 weeks of correct practice you will begin to notice some very nice benefits including an increase in stamina and mobility and a decrease in menstrual pain.

BUILDING
PHYSICAL CONSTITUTION

KIDNEY MERIDIAN
BEGINS THE CYCLE OF CHI
THROUGH THE MERIDIAN SYSTEM

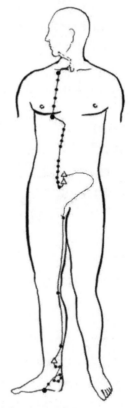

KIDNEY MERIDIAN

In TCM (Traditional Chinese Medicine) there are several different competing ideas and schools of thought about how many and the locations of some of the meridians and the pressure points. However, it is generally agreed that the Kidney Meridian is the mother or sequentially begins the cycle of Chi through the energy system in the body.

The Kidney Meridian begins in the middle hollow part on the bottom of the foot designated as the $KI\,1$ also known as the Yong Quan (Bubbling Well point) and continues up through the body to $KI\,27$ on the top of the chest in the hollow spot just below the collar bone. From there it goes up to the root of the tongue. Because of the Kidney Meridian's pathway from the bottom of the foot to the root of the tongue and man's natural connection to the earth (via gravity) the Kidney Meridian is in the best position to bring earth energy into the body. From there the Kidney Meridian moves the energy up into the body and the energy circulates into and through the rest of the meridians. The important point to note here for Chi Kung purposes is that, similar to the way that good quality deep breathing oxygenates the blood and moves the oxygen through the circulatory system, if I can do a better job of collecting energy with the Kidney Meridian then I will have more and better energy to circulate through the rest of my body courtesy of the meridian system.

KIDNEY BREATHING

Kidney Breathing is considered to be a very high level Chi Kung. In advanced practice kidney breathing can be done by directing the energy with the mind alone. However, for beginners and even intermediate practitioners it is much more practical and easier to <u>physically</u> facilitate the process of Kidney Breathing. The practitioner is not ready for advanced practice until after the physical method has been completely mastered and is easy to do such that the movement pathway of the energy is easily felt and fully understood from personal experience and practice.

There are various and different physical ways and methods to practice Kidney Breathing. The easiest to way to practice Kidney Breathing correctly is to do wall squats. I recommend that you begin by first doing regular squats and building up to 25 – 30 repetitions. Then, once this has been accomplished, begin doing wall squats. I will begin with a word or two on the value of squats. Then, Wall Squatting will be addressed in the next chapter.

SQUATS

Some physical conditioning experts consider the squat to be the "King of all Exercises". I have included a section on squats in this book because there are a fair amount of Chi Kung exercises that utilize squatting and I believe that if more people understood the real value of this exercise they would more likely make it a part of their daily routine. If you are already practicing the Carry the Cauldron exercise without difficulty then you are well on your way. Please read this complete section and the section on Wall Squats before attempting to practice squatting and please get proper instruction and or assistance from a professional instructor prior to practicing squats. Everyone who can do squats should do squats; but you have to do them correctly and safely!

If you were to pick just one simple physical exercise to condition yourself, the squat would provide the greatest overall benefit. Performed properly and safely the squat can be a very rewarding exercise for most people. Squats are an excellent way to energize your body and combat the effects of sitting. If you are able to add squats into your daily routine many of you will start to notice that your breathing, strength, flexibility, digestion, elimination, energy, appearance and concentration will all improve.

The many benefits of the squat include increased cardiovascular health, balance, endurance, stability, agility, flexibility, strength in the lower back, obliques, abdomen, leg strength, speed and increased bone density in the legs and hips to help prevent osteoporosis and possible broken bones and fractures. Improved respiration of working tissues used in the squat improves pumping of body fluids, aiding in removal of waste and delivery of nutrition to all tissues, including organs and glands. Squats make waste elimination faster, easier and more complete by improving and helping the movement of feces through the colon resulting in more regular bowel movements and helps prevent "fecal stagnation", a major cause of colon cancer, diverticulitis, inflammatory bowel syndrome and inflammatory bowel disease. Squats also build core strength and help promote healthy weight loss.

One of the most important benefits of squatting is the effect it has on the digestion and waste elimination process. In a natural and healthy situation fecal matter must move through the colon to be expelled from the body. The colon has several major parts worth mentioning the cecum, the ascending colon, the transverse colon, the descending colon, the sigmoid colon and the rectum. The ascending colon is called ascending because fecal matter has to move up through it against gravity before moving on to the transverse colon. Proper squats help with this process by automatically massaging the lower abdominal area with the thighs when you are at the lowest position in the squat. There are some who advocate always using the squat position to defecate because they say that this is how our body is naturally made and that the modern position of sitting on the toilet is the reason for many of the bowel diseases that occur in the world today.

Squats increase core strength for several reasons. Squats are a free-body movement that requires the use of almost every muscle in the body working together so that you can lower and raise your center of gravity. This includes the erectors (lower spinal muscles), glutes, abdominal muscles, quadriceps, calf muscles and hamstrings which are the largest and strongest muscles of the body. As a result squats are naturally "anabolic" (increasing testosterone and growth hormone production) and thereby adding more lean muscle mass. Squats are one of the best anabolic exercises. No other exercise stimulates as much overall muscle growth as the squat does.

WEIGHT LOSS

- Because squats exercise all the biggest and major muscles of the human body they create more demand for energy production thus energy expenditure is far greater when squatting than during any other exercise.

- Squats make it easier to control your weight after losing excess fat because the exercise increases muscle mass for improved body composition by adding more lean body weight compared to fat weight.

- This raises the metabolism making it easier to burn calories and keep fat off making for potentially faster weight loss and burning a higher percentage of fat while at rest.

Adding more lean muscle mass is the **best way to naturally increase the metabolic rate** and burn a higher percentage of fat while at rest.

Squats add beneficial physiological stress to your hormonal system. Properly performed breathing squats actually shift the body away from sympathetic (fight or flight) nervous system dominance & encourage parasympathetic (relaxing, calming and regenerating) activity. This aids in tissue repair and cultivation of Chi life-force energy.

How to Practice Squats

Proper form being critical to attaining its benefits, the proper squat is done with the head, shoulders and spine straightly aligned and the feet flat on the ground. The butt should be close to the ground but not touching. Make sure you go as low into the squat as you can without discomfort. To add squats to your daily routine start by doing a few a day and safely build your way up to 10 as soon as you can. Then build up to doing 30-50 squats a day. Also, you can practice in intervals throughout the day so that you are not overdoing it all at once. You must maintain a very erect body position when descending into the deep squat position. Leaning too far forward in the squat can be dangerous to your lower back. You should also learn how to go down into the squat position so you are low enough. Sink as low as possible. Ideally your rear will almost touch the floor.

For beginners I recommend relaxing and letting the body drop and let the air out of your body as if letting the air out of a balloon on the way down

and then pulling air deep into the belly/lungs on the way up as if the force of breathing in is what is lifting you up.

According to one of my teachers a few squats a day or even as little as one practiced extra slow -going down on a slow count of 20 and also rising up to a slow count of 20 will impart great physical development to the practitioner.   I utilize very slow and continuous Tai Chi speed to practice this and I like the mindset I use when practicing Carry the Cauldron in that I am constantly moving and breathing with no unnecessary tension in the movement and with relaxed slow continuous breathing.

It is amazing to me how much benefit this one simple exercise can impart when it is correctly practiced.

WALL SQUATTING

Wall squatting is the primary exercise taught at a Chi Kung hospital in China that is commonly referred to as "Curing the Incurables" Hospital because it is known for people going there and getting cured after they have been told by other medical facilities in China that there is no hope for them and that they are going to die. The Curing the Incurables hospital has helped quite a few people overcome impossible odds to get well. Information about this hospital and Grandmaster Pang Ming, M.D. have been brought to the U.S. by Luke Chan and detailed in his book 101 Miracles of Healing.

Grandmaster Pang Ming, M.D. is the founder of the Huaxia Zhineng Qigong Center, the world's largest medicineless hospital. As well as teaching the patients Chi Kung for themselves the Doctors at this facility are all Medical Chi Kung Masters and transmit energy to the patients to help them heal. I have film footage from this hospital where several of the Doctors, at the same time, transmit energy to a cancer patient and direct energy to facilitate the diminishing of the cancer. By directing their energy the Chi Kung Doctors cause the patient to go into remission within 15 minutes, in real time, while the cancer area is being viewed on a MRI. You actually see the cancer size fluctuate and diminish until it is completely gone.

We teach this method of healing energy transmission at our National Headquarters in Maryville, Tennessee located in the foothills of the Great Smoky Mountains.

To practice Wall Squatting, stand in front of a smooth wall and put the front of your toes up next to the wall and do a squat all the way down and then back up (see pictures on page 119). You will really have to relax on the way down and on the way back up in order not to fall over. You can put your forehead and nose on the wall to help and keep your hands/arms next to the wall as well. Hollow your chest and Relax your shoulders. On the way up picture that Wu Chi exercise #1 Hang from the invisible thread bungee cord/string (page 40) is gently lifting you up. Work towards being able to do this exercise 100 times per day for 100 days or more.

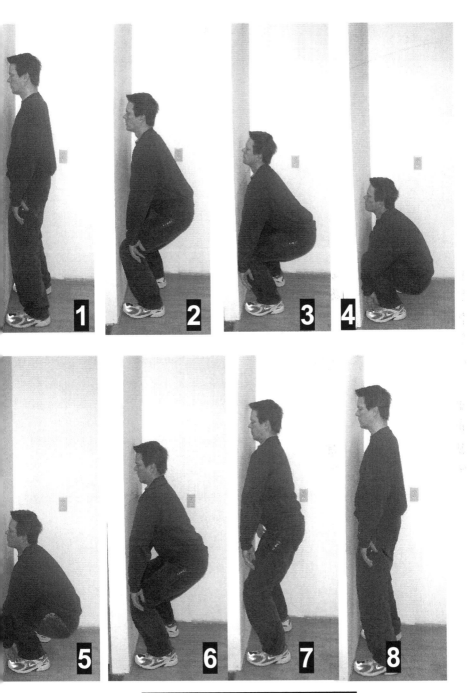

WALL SQUATTING

CONDENSING ENERGY (PACKING CHI)

After you have successfully developed the ability to activate, cultivate and circulate Chi then the next step is to balance, align and store Chi. Then, after you have mastered this process you will want to condense the energy into your bone marrow so that you will have it as part of long term health and for higher level jing power generation. A slang way to refer to this practice is to say "Pack Chi". As with most of the practices in this book there are a variety of ways to do this work. I have included here one of my favorite ways from Tai Chi to Pack Chi. Please make sure that you are fairly skilled at every other practice in this book before trying to Pack Chi. Also, do not confuse Bone Marrow Washing and Breathing with Packing Chi. These practices are quite different. You should NEVER push or tense while practicing Bone Marrow Washing and practicing with to much tension is the only way that the Bone Marrow Washing method presented in this book can hurt you.

A Tai Chi exercise that is excellent for Packing Chi is commonly known as Roll Back and Push. If you practice the Roll Back and Push exercise to Pack Chi to early in your development the good news is that it will not energetically hurt you. Instead, you will simply be wasting your time.

Roll Back and Push

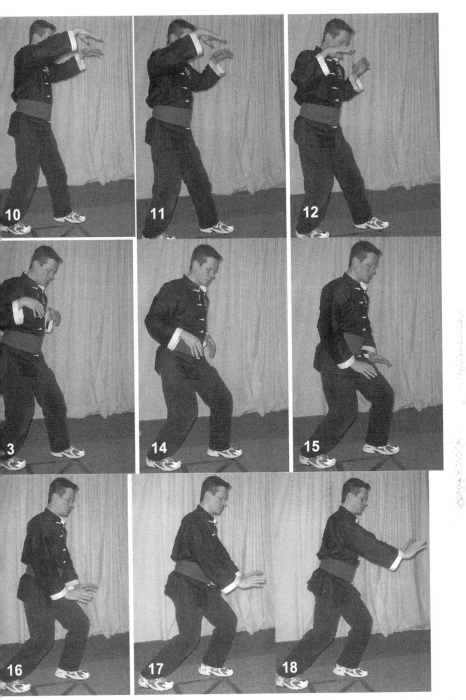

Repeat and Continue for as many repetitions as desired.

Roll Back and Push
Instructions

1. Visualize that you are pushing a canoe off of a sandy beach out into the water in one push. Push slow and strongly and for the full distance so that you can get the canoe all the way into the water in one push. Start with your weight on the back foot. As you push shift your weight to the front foot and push with your back leg the same way that you would push a stalled car out of the road.

2. At the end of the push then push a little extra with your hands and fingers.

3. Then, let the hands float upwards the way that they would once you lose contact with the canoe. You may get a slight tingling sensation or vibration in your hands and fingers.

4. While your hands are gently floating back towards your body then Roll back so that your weight shifts from the front foot back to the back foot.

5. When your hands get back to you then let them easily fall down the front of your body and sink your body weight in preparation for the next push.

6. Continue and repeat as desired.

7. Do at least three Carry the Cauldron and three Grand Tai Chi exercises (Chi Kung exercises on pages 69-76) to finish the Roll Back and Push Chi Kung.

Epilogue

It is my sincere hope and desire that this book proves to be useful and helpful in building your personal understanding and development of Chi energy cultivation, activation and circulation (flow). Many of the practices, techniques and methods presented in this book are the foundational energetics taught at the beginning of many of my Chi Kung programs for students training for physical, mental and spiritual health and self defense. These foundational practices are a solid base from which to begin and most of the more advanced practices build from these with the assumption that these principles have been practiced and are fully understood by the practitioner.

The next step in training, from this point, is to gain some basic knowledge about the primary Tai Chi moves and to work most of the energetics while practicing a basic form of Tai Chi. A basic 8 move Tai Chi set and practicing the Tai Chi set while simultaneously working some of the energetics presented in this book is the subject of the next book in this series.

Most of the energetics taught in this book will be practiced while the moves in the Tai Chi set are being performed. So, once the energetics are truly understood by the practitioner then the Tai Chi set will be used to practice the energetics and some of the more technical methods presented in this text will be replaced by proper practice of the Tai Chi. Proper practice refers to the principle that the body mechanics and the energetics are the most important aspect of the Tai Chi and that the physical moves are simply the vehicle to get you to the higher levels of practice. Exercise caution in graduating your practice and make sure that you do not try to move ahead to soon. Trying to move forward to soon will result in a lot of wasted effort and time and will prove detrimental to your long term goals.

The way to gain the understanding of the energetics is to practice the Chi Kung exercises and methods presented in this book. Please bear in mind that if you can not work and feel the energetics in the individual practice method or techniques presented in this text then it will be nearly impossible to get the energetics while performing the Tai Chi set. The ability to perform many of the energetics at the same time will also come from truly understanding the energetics presented in this book.

If you practice another system of Chi Kung, Tai Chi or other internal martial art then you may already have studied some of the energetics presented here but with different physical movements and/or methods. Try the exercises presented in this text and see how the energetics compare to what you do now. If it is different then make sure to gain the understanding of what is different and why it is different. This will help you to gain the understanding of the energetics and enhance your practice.

After the moves of the basic 8 move set of Tai Chi have been learned then the practice of the energetics will be incorporated into the Tai Chi practice. Then, some of the more advanced practices include learning to feel the Chi flow through your body and various Jing expressions can be learned. This includes utilizing different kinds of mind intent and spiritual energy. The benefits of such practice are many and will be taught to our more advanced students.

Advanced skills include but are not limited to Empty Force, the Mind Hit, Healing oneself by manipulation of the internal energy inside your own body, Iron

Body/Golden Bell Covered, healing others with your mind and spirit without physical contact, becoming the calm in the eye of the storm so that you can achieve immediate calm and using your mind and spirit to also calm others, being able to energetically perceive and correct physical and energetic imbalances in others with psychic sight, automatically perceiving the mind intent of others (basic mind reading at a very functional level of skill) and many other uncommon and unusual high level skills that are seldom seen in the Western world.

Sigung Richard Clear is an internationally recognized Sigung (Master) of Tai Chi and Chi Kung. Sigung Clear studied Tai Chi & Chi Kung both in the U.S. and China. Master Clear began his study of Tai Chi at a very young age after it was discovered that he had inherited a physical form of degenerative arthritis. He experiences no pain from the arthritis and is more supple than most people half his age.

Sigung Clear is a 3rd generation lineage holder in Tai Chi from Lee Ying Arng who was a senior student under Yang Chen Fu. Tyrone Jackson was Dr Wu's senior disciple. Sigung Clear also studied directly with famous

Yang Chen Fu
|
Lee Ying Arng
|
Dr Fred Wu
|
Tyrone Jackson
|
Richard Clear

masters such as Ma Yeuh Liang, Wen Mei Yu, Ju Bong Yi, Pei Xi Rong, Willem de Thouars and Don Ethan Miller among others. Sigung Clear began teaching in 1985 and has over 30 years of continuous study in Tai Chi, Martial Arts, Psychology, Philosophy, Alternative Medicine & Physiology.

Sigung Clear's Tai Chi has been featured in national magazines and on television. He has a practical teaching method rooted in the basics and knows both the healing & the martial side of Tai Chi and Chi Kung in depth. He holds a Masters Level (Si Gung) in Internal Kung fu and is a senior instructor in several martial arts.

CLEAR'S TAI CHI
CERTIFICATION PROGRAM

All Videos available in DVD or VHS

Chi Energy
Activation, Cultivation & Flow
(Book and Video)   - $75

Clear's Tai Chi Big 8 Set   Video   - $45

Clear's Tai Chi 13   Video   - $45

Basic Skills Tape 1   Video   - $75

Basic Skills Tape 2   Video   - $75

Sticky Hands and Push Hands Video
(Emphasis on the Push Hands)   - $50

Basic Self Defense Applications A   - $75
                              Video
Basic Self Defense Applications B   - $75
                              Video
Freestyle Self Defense
& Push Hands Games Intro   Video   - $75

Total $590.00
- Discount $95.00
and

Add Free Shipping
and Nei Kung Tape
Discount Bonuses = Over $200 value

Total Cost if purchased all at once $495.00

Testing – Form Correction
– Evaluation (Video or Live) $150.00

www.clearstaichi.com

132

Made in the USA
Middletown, DE
30 August 2015